Watch It Grow

Snail

Barrie Watts

FRANKLIN WATTS
LONDON•SYDNEY

First published in 2002 by Franklin Watts
96 Leonard Street, London EC2A 4XD

Franklin Watts Australia
56 O'Riordan Street, Alexandria, NSW 2015

© Barrie Watts 2002

Editor: Adrian Cole
Art director: Jonathan Hair
Photographer: Barrie Watts
Illustrator: David Burroughs
Consultant: Beverley Mathias, REACH

A CIP catalogue record for this book
is available from the British Library

ISBN 0 7496 4431 1

Dewey Classification 594

Printed in Hong Kong, China

How to use this book

Watch It Grow has been specially designed to cater for a range of reading and learning abilities. Initially children may just follow the pictures. Ask them to describe in their own words what they see. Other children will enjoy reading the single sentence in large type, in conjunction with the pictures. This single sentence is then expanded in the main text. More adept readers will be able to follow the text and pictures by themselves through to the conclusion of the life cycle.

Contents

Snails come from eggs. 4

The eggs hatch. 6

The baby snail eats its first meal. 8

The young snail leaves its nest. 10

The shell changes. 12

The snail eats with its tongue. 14

The snail is six months old. 16

The snail hides. 18

The shell grows stronger. 20

The snail moves slowly. 22

The snail is fully grown. 24

The adults mate. 26

The snail lays eggs. 28

Word bank 30

Life cycle 31

Index 32

Snails come from eggs.

Snail eggs are white and each one is about the size of a match head. The eggs have a soft, tough shell that protects the young as they develop inside.

During the summer months an adult snail lays up to 100 eggs. The eggs need warmth for the baby snails to grow and hatch out.

The eggs hatch.

After two weeks, the white eggs begin to change colour. Inside, a tiny snail is ready to hatch out. The soft eggshell gets thinner until it falls apart.

The young snail is born with its own soft, thin shell. It is a very pale colour. The young snail will grow to look like its parents.

The baby snail eats its first meal.

The first thing the newly-hatched snail does is look for food. It starts with its own eggshell and then it eats any other empty shells it finds in the nest.

For the first few days, the young snail stays in the nest and finds food in the soil nearby. It can only eat tiny pieces of plants and leaves, because its mouth is very small.

The young snail leaves its nest.

Four days after hatching, the young snail's shell is still soft. It has eaten all the food it can find, and must now leave the warm, safe nest.

The snail makes its way above ground. It will spend most of its life alone. It will only come together with other snails for **mating** and **hibernating**.

Snails are plant-eaters. They only come out to feed when it is cool and damp. At night, the darkness hides snails from **predators** that might eat them.

The shell changes.

Two weeks after hatching, the shell of
the young snail has changed colour.

The shell
is getting
stronger and harder.
It curls round in a spiral as it
grows. Each turn of the spiral
is called a **whorl**.

The snail builds its shell from a
chalky substance, called **calcium**.
It gets the calcium from the food
it eats. The shell is the snail's
home. It protects the snail from
predators and bad weather.

The snail eats with its tongue.

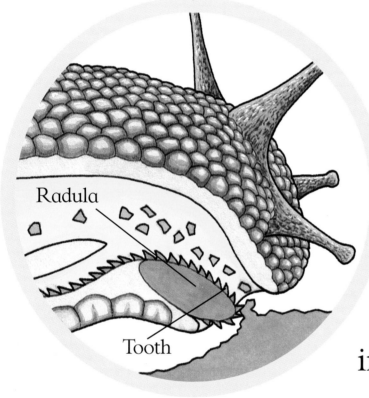

Radula

Tooth

A snail cannot bite or chew food. It uses its tongue, called a **radula**, to scrape food into its mouth.

The radula is like a grater with hundreds of tiny, sharp teeth. These teeth never wear out because they are always growing.

The snail is six months old.

Six months after hatching, the snail's body has changed colour. It has three **whorls** and is about half the size of its parents.

Look closely at a snail shell and you can see growth lines on it. Growth lines form ridges that are made when the snail stops and starts feeding. This is because the shell only grows when the snail is feeding.

The snail hides.

During the day and in dry weather, the snail hides away. It finds a damp, shady place - under a stone or a rotting log.

The snail does not like the sun because the heat dries out its body. If this happens, the snail will die.

The snail seals itself into its shell with a layer of slime. This stops water escaping from its body. The snail breathes through a tiny air hole.

In the winter, groups of snails come together to **hibernate** in a sheltered place. They can stay sealed in their shells for many months.

The shell grows stronger.

By the time the snail is nine months old, its shell has four **whorls**.

An adult snail has two layers to its shell. The inner layer is very strong and hard. It is protected by the outer layer which is thin and almost **transparent**.

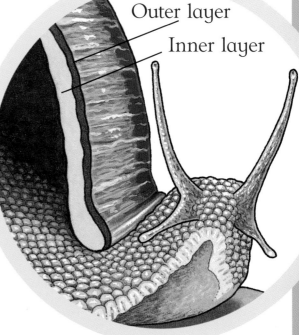

Outer layer

Inner layer

The snail makes the outer layer first. It can only start to make the inner layer when it is a few weeks old and has eaten enough food.

The snail moves slowly.

After nine months the snail is almost fully grown. Although it is much bigger now, it cannot move any quicker than a baby snail. It travels very slowly, creeping along on a carpet of slippery slime.

The slime is made by
a part of the snail's
foot and is very sticky.
The slime allows snails
to climb up or down.

The snail is fully grown.

After one year the snail is fully grown. Although the shell does not get any bigger, it is thicker.

Inside the shell, the snail's body has slowly changed until it has become an adult.

On a warm summer night, the snail looks for a partner with whom to **mate**.

The adults mate.

Before two snails **mate**, they take part in a special **courtship dance**. Adult snails are both male and female. They cling together and exchange packets of **sperm** that **fertilise** their eggs. When the **fertilised** eggs are laid they will become baby snails.

The eggs are usually laid two weeks after **mating**. However, the **sperm** can be stored for over a year in the snails' bodies until the eggs are ready.

The snail lays eggs.

When the snail is ready to lay its eggs, it finds a suitable place in moist soil and makes a small nest.

One by one, the snail slowly pushes the eggs out of its body through an opening behind its head.

A snail does not always lay all its eggs at the same time. It may make another nest and lay some more a few weeks later.

Once the snail has laid its eggs, it leaves them. After about two weeks, baby snails will hatch out from the eggs.

Word bank

Calcium - A chalky substance the snail obtains from the food it eats. We also get calcium from food such as milk. It makes our teeth and bones stronger.

Courtship dance - This is a special dance performed by some animals when they find a partner. It takes place before snails mate and can last several hours.

Fertilise - Eggs are fertilised when they are brought into contact with sperm. This usually happens during mating.

Hibernating - When an animal hides away for the winter because it is cold. Snails hibernate by sealing themselves into their shells.

Mating - This happens when two snails join together and exchange sperm packets that will fertilise their eggs.

Radula - A snail's tongue which it uses to grate food.

Sperm - The male cells needed to fertilise eggs. Every adult snail carries these cells.

Transparent - When something is clear, like glass in a window, it is called transparent.

Whorl - Each spiral on a snail's shell is called a whorl.

Life cycle

An adult snail
lays some eggs.

Usually after two
weeks the snails
lay their eggs.

After two
weeks
the eggs
hatch.

The snails dance
before they mate.

Four days later
the baby snail
looks for food.

After one year the
snail is fully grown. It
looks for a partner.

Two weeks after
hatching the snail's
shell gets stronger.

The snail moves
around on a
layer of slime.

Index

calcium 13
colour 6, 12, 16
courtship dance 26

eggs 4, 5, 6, 26, 27, 28, 29

fertilise *or* fertilised 26
food 8, 9, 10, 13, 14, 21

growth lines 17

hatch 5, 6, 29
hibernate *or* hibernating 10, 19

mate *or* mating 10, 25, 26, 27

nest 8, 9, 10, 28, 29

predators 11, 13

radula 14

shell 4, 7, 8, 10, 12, 13, 17, 19, 20, 25
slime 19, 22, 23
sperm 26, 27

transparent 20

whorl 13, 16, 20